ABE LINCOLN
Gets His Chance

By FRANCES CAVANAH

Illustrated by Don Sibley

SCHOLASTIC INC.
New York Toronto London Auckland Sydney

ISBN 0-590-08501-8

12 11   6 7 8 9/8 0 1/9

Printed in the U.S.A.   11

In writing this story of Abraham Lincoln, the author depended primarily on Lincoln's own statements and on the statements of his family and friends who had firsthand knowledge of his everyday life. In instances when dialogue had to be imagined, the conversation might logically have taken place in the light of known circumstances. Such descriptive details as were necessarily added were based on authentic accounts of pioneer times.

F.C.

CHAPTER *ONE*

THERE WAS A NEW BOY BABY at the Lincoln cabin! By cracky! thought Dennis Hanks as he hurried up the path, he was going to like having a boy cousin. They could go swimming together. Maybe they could play Indian. Dennis pushed open the cabin door.

"Where is he?" he shouted. "Where is he?"

"Sh!" A neighbor, who had come in to help, put her finger to her lips. "The baby is asleep."

Nancy Lincoln was lying on the pole bed in a corner of the one-room house. She looked very white under the dark bearskin covering, but when she heard Dennis she raised her head. "It's all right, Denny," she said. "You can see him now."

Dennis tiptoed over to the bed. A small bundle, wrapped in a homespun shawl, rested in the curve of Nancy's arm. When she pulled back the shawl, Dennis could not think of anything to say. The baby was so wrinkled and so red. It looked just like a cherry after the juice had been squeezed out.

Nancy touched one of the tiny hands with the tip of her finger. "See his wee red fists and the way he throws them around!" she said.

"What's his name?" Dennis asked at last.

"We're calling him after his grandpappy: Abraham Lincoln!"

"That great big name for that scrawny little mite?"

Nancy sounded hurt. "Give him a chance to grow, will you?"

Then she saw that Dennis was only teasing. "You wait!" she went on. "It won't be long before Abe will

2

be running around in buckskin breeches and a coonskin cap."

"Well, maybe —"

The door opened and Tom Lincoln, the baby's father, came in. With him was Aunt Betsy Sparrow. She kissed Nancy and carried the baby over to a stool by the fireplace. Making little cooing noises under her breath, she dressed him in a white shirt and a yellow flannel petticoat. Sally Lincoln, two years old, who did not know quite what to make of the new brother, came over and stood beside her. Dennis drew up another stool and watched.

Aunt Betsy looked across at him and smiled. Dennis, an orphan, lived with her, and she knew that he was often lonely. There weren't many people living in Kentucky in the year 1809, and Dennis had no boys to play with.

"I reckon you're mighty tickled to have a new cousin," she said.

"I — I guess so," said Dennis slowly.

"Want to hold him?"

Dennis was not quite sure whether he did or not. Before he could answer, Aunt Betsy laid the baby in his arms. Sally edged closer. She started to put out her hand, but pulled it back. Abraham was so small that she was afraid to touch him.

"Don't you fret, Sally," said Dennis. "Cousin Nancy said that he is going to grow. And when he does, do you know what I'm going to do? I'm going to teach him to swim."

Looking down into the tiny red face, Dennis felt a sudden warm glow in his heart. "Yes, and we can go fishing down at the creek. When I go to the mill to get the corn ground, he can come along. He can ride behind me on the horse, and when it goes cloppety-clop — "

Dennis swung the baby back and forth. It puckered up its face and began to cry. Dennis caught his breath in dismay. How could such a large noise come out of such a small body?

"Here, Aunt, take him quick!"

He looked at Cousin Nancy out of the corner of his

eye. "I reckon he'll never come to much."

"Now, Dennis Hanks, I want you to behave," said Aunt Betsy, but this time Nancy paid no attention to his teasing. She held out her arms for her son and cuddled him against her breast.

"As I told you," she said gaily, "you have to give him a chance to grow."

It was almost dark by the time Aunt Betsy had tidied the one-room cabin. She cooked some dried berries for Nancy and fed Sally. Dennis begged to spend the night. After his aunt had put on her shawl and left for her own cabin, he curled up in a bearskin on the floor.

"Denny," asked Nancy, "what day is this?"

"It's Sunday — "

"I mean what day of the month?"

"I don't rightly know, Cousin Nancy."

"I remember now," she went on. "It is the twelfth day of February. February 12, 1809! Little Abe's birthday!"

Outside the wind rose, whistling through the bare branches of the trees. There was a blast of cold air as the door opened. Tom came in, his arms piled high with wood. He knelt on the dirt floor to build up the

5

fire, and the rising flames lit the log walls with a faint red glow.

"Are you glad it's a boy, Tom?" Nancy asked as he lay down beside her. "I am."

"Yes," said Tom, but when she spoke to him again, he did not answer. He was asleep. She could see his tired face in the firelight. Life had been hard for Tom; it was hard for most pioneers. She hoped that their children would have things a little easier. The baby whimpered, and she held him closer.

Denny's voice piped up: "Cousin Nancy, will Abe ever grow to be as big as me?"

"Bigger'n you are now," she told him.

"Will he grow as big as Cousin Tom?"

"Bigger'n anybody, maybe."

Nancy looked down at her son, now peacefully asleep. She made a song for him, a song so soft it was almost a whisper: "Abe — Abe," she crooned. "Abe Lincoln, you be going to grow — and grow — and grow!"

CHAPTER *TWO*

Abraham Lincoln did grow. He seemed to grow bigger every day. By the time he was seven, he was as tall as his sister, although Sally was two years older. That fall their father made a trip up to Indiana.

"Why did Pappy go so far away?" Sally asked one afternoon.

"When is he coming home?" asked Abe.

"Pretty soon, most likely."

Nancy laid down her sewing and tried to explain. Their pa had had a hard time making a living for them. He was looking for a better farm. Tom was also a carpenter. Maybe some of the new settlers who were going to Indiana to live would give him work. Anyway, he thought that poor folks were better off up there.

Abe had looked surprised. He'd never thought about being poor. There were so many things that he liked to do in Kentucky. He liked to go swimming with Dennis after his chores were done. There were fish to be caught and caves to explore. He and Sally had had a chance to go to school for a few weeks. Abe could write his name, just like his father. He could read much better. Tom knew a few words, but his children could read whole sentences.

Abe leaned up against his mother. "Tell us the story with our names," he begged.

Nancy put her arm around him. She often told the children stories from the Bible. One of their favorites was about Abraham and Sarah. " 'Now the Lord said unto Abraham,' " she began — and stopped to listen.

The door opened, and Tom Lincoln stood grinning down at them. "Well, folks," he said, "we're moving to Indiany."

Nancy and the children, taken by surprise, asked questions faster than Tom could answer them. He had staked out a claim about a hundred miles to the north, at a place called Pigeon Creek. He was buying the land from the Government and could take his time to pay for it. He wanted to start for Indiana at once, before the weather got any colder.

It did not take long to get ready. A few possessions — a skillet, several pans, the water buckets, the fire shovel, a few clothes, a homespun blanket, a patchwork quilt, and several bearskins — were packed on the back of one of the horses. Nancy and Sally rode on the other horse. Abe and his father walked. At night they camped along the way.

When at last they reached the Ohio River, Abe stared in surprise. It was so blue, so wide, so much bigger than the creek where he and Dennis had gone swimming. There were so many boats. One of them, a long low raft, was called a ferry. The Lincolns went right on board with their pack horses, and it carried them across the shining water to the wooded shores of Indiana.

Indiana was a much wilder place than Kentucky. There was no road leading to Pigeon Creek — only a path through the forest. It was so narrow that sometimes Tom had to clear away some underbrush before they could go on. Or else he had to stop to cut down a tree that stood in their way. Abe, who was big and strong for his age, had his own little ax. He helped his father all he could.

Fourteen miles north of the river, they came to a cleared place in the forest. Tom called it his "farm." He hastily put up a shelter — a camp made of poles and brush and leaves — where they could stay until he had time to build a cabin. It had only three walls. The fourth side was left open, and in this open space Tom built a fire. The children helped their mother to unpack, and she mixed batter for corn bread in a big iron skillet. She cut up a squirrel that Tom had shot earlier in the day, and cooked it over the campfire.

"Now if you will fetch me your plates," she said, "we'll have our supper."

The plates were only slabs of bark. On each slab Nancy put a piece of fried squirrel and a hunk of corn bread. The children sank down on one of the bearskins to eat their first meal in their new home. By this time it was quite dark. They could see only a few feet beyond the circle of light made by their campfire.

Nancy shivered. She knew that they had neighbors. Tom had told her there were seven other families living at Pigeon Creek. But the trees were so tall, the night so black, that she had a strange feeling that they were the only people alive for miles around.

"Don't you like it here, Mammy?" Abe asked. To him this camping out was an adventure, but he wanted his mother to like it, too.

"I'm just feeling a little cold," she told him.

"I like it," said Sally decidedly. "But it is sort of scary. Are you scared, Abe?"

"Me?" Abe stuck out his chest. "What is there to be scared of?"

At that moment a long-drawn-out howl came from the forest. Another seemed to come from just beyond their campfire. Then another and another — each howl louder and closer. The black curtain of the night was pierced by two green spots of light. The children huddled against their mother, but Tom Lincoln laughed.

"I reckon I know what you're scared of: a wolf."

"A wolf?" Sally shrieked.

"Yep. See its green eyes. But it won't come near our fire."

He got up and threw on another log. As the flames blazed higher, the green lights disappeared. There was a crashing sound in the underbrush.

"Hear him running away? Cowardly varmint!" Tom

sat down again. "No wolf will hurt us if we keep our fire going."

It was a busy winter. Abe worked side by side with his father. "How that boy can chop!" thought Nancy, as she heard the sound of his ax biting into wood. Tree after tree had to be cut down before crops could be planted. With the coming of spring, he helped his father plow the stumpy ground. He learned to plow a straight furrow. He planted seeds in the furrows.

In the meantime, some of the neighbors helped Tom build a cabin. It had one room, with a tiny loft above. The floor was packed-down dirt. There were no windows. The only door was a long, up-and-down hole cut in one wall and covered by a bearskin. But Tom had made a table and several three-legged stools, and there was a pole bed in one corner. Nancy was glad to be living in a real house again, and she kept it neat and clean.

She was no longer lonely. Aunt Betsy and her husband, Uncle Thomas, brought Dennis with them from Kentucky to live in the shelter near the Lincoln cabin. Several other new settlers arrived, settlers with children. A school master, Andrew Crawford, decided to start a school.

"Maybe you'll have a chance to go, Abe," Nancy

told him. "You know what the schoolmaster down in Kentucky said. He said you were a learner."

Abe looked up at her and smiled. He was going to like living in Indiana!

CHAPTER *THREE*

But sad days were coming to Pigeon Creek. There was a terrible sickness. Aunt Betsy and Uncle Thomas died, and Dennis came to live with the Lincolns. Then Nancy was taken ill. After she died, her family felt that nothing would ever be the same again.

Sally tried to keep house, but she was only twelve. The one little room and the loft above looked dirtier and more and more gloomy as the weeks went by. Sally found that cooking for four people was not easy. The smoke from the fireplace got into her eyes. Some days Tom brought home a rabbit or a squirrel for her to fry. On other days, it was too cold to go hunting. Then there was only corn bread to eat, and Sally's corn bread wasn't very good.

It was hard to know who missed Nancy more — Tom or the children. He sat around the cabin looking cross and glum. The ground was frozen, so very little work could be done on the farm. He decided, when Andrew Crawford started his school, that Abe and Sally might as well go. There was nothing else for them to do, and Nancy would have wanted it.

For the first time since his mother's death, Abe seemed to cheer up. Every morning, except when there were chores to do at home, he and Sally took a path through the woods to the log schoolhouse. Master Crawford kept a "blab" school. The "scholars," as he called his pupils, studied their lessons out loud. The louder they shouted, the better he liked it. If a scholar didn't know his lesson, he had to stand in the corner with a long pointed cap on his head. This was called a "duncecap."

One boy who never had to wear a duncecap was Abe Lincoln. He was too smart. His side won nearly every spelling match. He was good at figuring, and he had the best handwriting of anyone at school. Master Crawford taught reading from the Bible, but he had several other books from which he read aloud. Among Abe's favorite stories were the ones about some wise animals that talked. They were by a man named Aesop who lived hundreds of years before.

Abe even made up compositions of his own. He called them "sentences." One day he found some of the boys being cruel to a terrapin, or turtle. He made them stop. Then he wrote a composition in which he said that animals had feelings the same as folks.

Sometimes Abe's sentences rhymed. There was one rhyme that the children thought was a great joke:

> Abe Lincoln, his hand and pen,
> He will be good, but God knows when.

"That Abe Lincoln is funny enough to make a cat laugh," they said.

They always had a good time watching Abe during the class in "manners." Once a week Master Crawford had them practice being ladies and gentlemen. One scholar would pretend to be a stranger who had just arrived in Pigeon Creek. He would leave the school-house, come back, and knock at the door. Another scholar would greet "the stranger," lead him around the room, and introduce him.

One day it was Abe's turn to do the introducing. He opened the door to find his best friend, Nat Grigsby, waiting outside. Nat bowed low, from the waist. Abe bowed. His buckskin trousers, already too short, slipped up still farther, showing several inches of his bare leg. He looked so solemn that some of the girls giggled. The schoolmaster frowned and pounded on his desk. The giggling stopped.

"Master Crawford," said Abe, "this here is Mr. Grigsby. His pa just moved to these parts. He figures on coming to your school."

Andrew Crawford rose and bowed. "Welcome," he said. "Mr. Lincoln, introduce Mr. Grigsby to the other scholars."

The children sat on two long benches made of split logs. Abe led Nat down the length of the front bench. Each girl rose and made a curtsy. Nat bowed. Each boy rose and bowed. Nat returned the bow. Abe kept saying funny things under his breath that the school-master could not hear. But the children heard, and they could hardly keep from laughing out loud.

Sally sat on the second bench. "Mrs. Lincoln," said Abe in a high falsetto voice, "this here be Mr. Grigsby."

While she was making her curtsy, Sally's cheeks suddenly grew red. "Don't let on I told you, Mr. Grigsby," Abe whispered, "but Mrs. Lincoln bakes the worst corn bread of anyone in Pigeon Creek."

Sally forgot that they were having a lesson in manners. "Don't you dare talk about my corn bread," she said angrily.

The little log room rocked with laughter. This time Master Crawford had also heard Abe's remark. He walked over to the corner where he kept a bundle of switches. He picked one up and laid it across his desk.

"We'll have no more monkeyshines," he said severely. "Go on with the introducing."

One day Abe almost got into real trouble. He had

started for school early, as he often did, so that he could read one of Master Crawford's books. He was feeling sad as he walked through the woods; he seemed to miss his mother more each day. When he went into the schoolhouse, he looked up and saw a pair of deer antlers. Master Crawford had gone hunting. He had shot a deer and nailed the antlers above the door.

What a wonderful place to swing! thought Abe. He leaped up and caught hold of the prongs. He began swinging back and forth.

CRASH! One prong came off in his hand, and he fell to the floor. He hurried to his seat, hoping that the master would not notice.

But Master Crawford was proud of those antlers. When he saw what had happened, he picked up the switch on his desk. It made a swishing sound as he swung it back and forth.

"Who broke my deer antlers?" he shouted.

No one answered. Abe hunched down as far as he could on the bench. He seemed to be trying to hide inside his buckskin shirt.

Master Crawford repeated his question. "Who broke my deer antlers? I aim to find out, if I have to thrash every scholar in this school."

All of the children looked scared, Abe most of all.

But he stood up. He marched up to Master Crawford's desk and held out the broken prong that he had been hiding in his hand.

"I did it, sir," he said. "I didn't mean to do it, but I hung on the antlers and they broke. I wouldn't have done it if I had thought they'd a broke."

The other scholars thought that Abe would get a licking. Instead, Master Crawford told him to stay in after school. They had a long talk. He liked Abe's honesty in owning up to what he had done. He knew how much he missed his mother. Perhaps he understood that sometimes a boy "cuts up" to try to forget how sad he feels.

Abe felt sadder than ever after Master Crawford moved away from Pigeon Creek. Then Tom Lincoln left. One morning he rode off on horseback without telling anyone where he was going. Several days went by. Even easygoing Dennis was worried when Tom did not return.

Abe did most of the chores. In the evening he practiced his sums. Master Crawford had taught him to do easy problems in arithmetic, and he did not want to forget what he had learned. He had no pen, no ink, not even a piece of paper. He took a burnt stick from the fireplace and worked his sums on a flat board.

He wished that he had a book to read. Instead, he tried to remember the stories that the schoolmaster had told. He repeated them to Sally and Dennis, as they huddled close to the fire to keep warm. He said them again to himself after he went to bed in the loft.

There were words in some of the stories that Abe did not understand. He tried to figure out what the words meant. He thought about the people in the stories. He thought about the places mentioned and wondered what they were like.

There were thoughts inside Abraham Lincoln's head that even Sally did not know anything about.

CHAPTER *FOUR*

ABE TOOK ANOTHER BITE of corn bread and swallowed hard. "Don't you like it?" asked Sally anxiously. "I know it doesn't taste like the corn bread Mammy used to make."

She looked around the room. The furniture was the same as their mother had used — a homemade table and a few three-legged stools. The same bearskin hung before the hole in the wall that was their only door. But Nancy had kept the cabin clean. She had known how to build a fire that didn't smoke. Sally glanced down at her faded linsey-woolsey dress, soiled with soot. The dirt floor felt cold to her bare feet. Her last pair of moccasins had worn out weeks ago.

"I don't mind the corn bread — at least, not much."

23

Abe finished his piece, down to the last crumb. "If I seem down in the mouth, Sally, it is just because —"

He walked over to the fireplace, where he stood with his back to the room.

"He misses Nancy," said Dennis bluntly, "the same as the rest of us. Then Tom has been gone for quite a spell."

Sally put her hand on Abe's shoulder. "I'm scared. Do you reckon something has happened to Pappy? Isn't he ever coming back?"

Abe stared into the fire. He was thinking of the wolves and panthers loose in the woods. There were many dangers for a man riding alone over the rough forest paths. The boy wanted to say something to comfort Sally, but he had to tell the truth. "I don't know, I —"

He stopped to listen. Few travelers passed by their cabin in the winter, but he was sure that he heard a faint noise in the distance. It sounded like the creak of wheels. The noise came again — this time much closer. A man's voice was shouting: "Get-up! Get-up!"

"Maybe it's Pappy!" Abe pushed aside the bearskin and rushed outside. Sally and Dennis were right behind him.

"It *is* Pappy," Sally cried. "But look —"

Tom Lincoln had left Pigeon Creek on horseback. He was returning in a wagon drawn by four horses. He was not alone. A strange woman sat beside him, holding a small boy in her lap. Two girls, one about Sally's age, the other about eight, stood behind her. The wagon was piled high with furniture — more furniture than the Lincoln children had ever seen.

"Whoa, there!" Tom Lincoln pulled at the reins and brought the wagon to a stop before the door.

"Here we are, Sarah." He jumped down and held out his hand to help the woman.

She was very neat-looking, tall and straight, with neat little curls showing at the edge of her brown hood. She said, "Tsch! Tsch!" when she saw Tom's children. She stared at their soiled clothing, their matted hair, their faces smudged with soot. "Tsch! Tsch!" she said again, and Abe felt hot all over, in spite of the cold wind. He dug the toe of his moccasin into the frozen ground.

"Abe! Sally!" their father said. "I've brought you a new mammy. This here is the Widow Johnston. That is, she *was* the Widow Johnston." He cleared his throat. "She is Mrs. Lincoln now. I've been back to Kentucky to get myself a wife."

"Howdy!" The new Mrs. Lincoln was trying to sound cheerful. She beckoned to the children in the wagon. They jumped down and stood beside her. "These here are my young ones," she went on. "The big gal is Betsy. The other one is Mathilda. This little shaver is Johnny."

Dennis came forward to be introduced, but he had eyes only for Betsy. She gave him a coy look out of her china-blue eyes. Tilda smiled shyly at Sally. Both of the Johnston girls wore pretty linsey-woolsey dresses under their shawls and neat moccasins on their feet. Sally, looking down at her own soiled dress and bare toes, wished that she could run away and hide. Abe said "Howdy" somewhere down inside his stomach.

Sarah, Tom's new wife, looked around the littered yard, then at the cabin. It did not even have a window! It did not have a door that would open and shut — only a ragged bearskin flapping in the wind. She had known Tom since he was a boy and had always liked him. Her first husband, Mr. Johnston, had died some time before, and when Tom had returned to Kentucky and asked her to marry him, she had said yes. He had told her that his children needed a mother's care, and he was right.

"Poor young ones!" she thought. Aloud she said, "Well, let's not all stand out here and freeze. Can't we go inside and get warm?"

The inside of the cabin seemed almost as cold as the outdoors, and even more untidy. Johnny clung to his mother's skirt and started to cry. He wanted to go back to Kentucky. His sisters peered through the gloom, trying to see in the dim light. Sally was sure that they were looking at her. She sat down hastily and tucked her feet as far back as she could under the stool. Abe stood quite still, watching this strange woman who had come without warning to take his mother's place.

She smiled at him. He did not smile back.

Slowly she turned and looked around. Her clear gray eyes took in every nook and crack of the miserable little one-room house. She noticed the dirty bearskins piled on the pole bed in the corner. She saw the pegs in the wall that led to the loft. The fire smoldering in the fireplace gave out more smoke than heat.

"The first thing we'd better do," she said, taking off

her bonnet, "is to build up that fire. Then we'll get some victuals ready. I reckon everybody will feel better when we've had a bite to eat."

From that moment things began to happen in the Lincoln cabin. Tom went out to the wagon to unhitch the horses. Dennis brought in more firewood. Abe and Mathilda started for the spring, swinging the water pail between them. Betsy mixed a fresh batch of corn bread in the iron skillet, and Sally set it on the hearth to bake. Tom came back from the wagon, carrying a comb of honey and a slab of bacon, and soon the magic smell of frying bacon filled the air. There were no dishes, but Sally kept large pieces of bark in the cupboard. Eight people sat down at the one little table, but no one seemed to mind that it was crowded.

The Lincoln children had almost forgotten how good bacon could taste. Abe ate in silence, his eyes on his plate. Sally seemed to feel much better. Sitting between her stepsisters, she was soon chattering with them as though they were old friends. Once she called the new Mrs. Lincoln "Mamma," just as Sarah's own children did. Dennis sat on the other side of Betsy. He seemed to be enjoying himself most of all. He sopped up his last drop of golden honey on his last piece of corn bread.

"I declare," he said, grinning, "we ain't had a meal like this since Nancy died."

Abe jumped up at the mention of his mother's name. He was afraid that he was going to cry. He had started for the door, when he felt his father's rough hand on his shoulder.

"Abe Lincoln, you set right down there and finish your corn bread."

Abe looked up at Tom out of frightened gray eyes. But he shook his head. "I can't, Pa."

"A nice way to treat your new ma!" Tom Lincoln sounded both angry and embarrassed. "You clean up your plate, or I'll give you a good hiding."

The young Johnstons gasped. Abe could hear Sally's whisper: "Please, Abe! Do as Pa says." Then he heard another voice.

"Let the boy be, Tom." It was Sarah Lincoln speaking.

There was something about the way she said it that made Abe decide to come back and sit down. He managed somehow to eat the rest of his corn bread. He looked up and saw that she was smiling at him again. He almost smiled back.

Sarah looked relieved. "Abe and I," she said, "are going to have plenty of chance to get acquainted."

CHAPTER *FIVE*

Sarah rose from the table. "There's a lot of work to be done here," she announced, "before we can bring in my plunder." She meant her furniture and other possessions in the wagon. "First, we'll need plenty of hot water. Who wants to go to the spring?"

She was looking at Abe. "I'll go, ma'am." He grabbed the water bucket and hurried through the door.

Abe made several trips to the spring that afternoon. Each bucketful of water that he brought back was poured into the big iron kettle over the fireplace. Higher and higher roared the flames. When Sarah wasn't asking for more water, she was asking for more wood. The steady chop-chop of Tom's ax could be heard from the wood lot.

Everyone was working, even Dennis. Sarah gave him a pan of soap and hot water and told him to wash the cabin walls. The girls scrubbed the table, the three-legged stools, and the corner cupboard inside and out. Sarah climbed the peg ladder to peer into the loft.

"Tsch! Tsch!" she said, when she saw the corn husks and dirty bearskins on which the boys had been sleeping. "Take them out and burn them, Tom."

"Burn them?" he protested.

"Yes, and burn the covers on the downstairs bed, too. I reckon I have enough feather beds and blankets to go around. We're starting fresh in this house. We'll soon have it looking like a different place."

Not since Nancy died had the cabin had such a thorough cleaning. Then came the most remarkable part of that remarkable afternoon — the unloading of the wagon. Sarah's pots and pans shone from much scouring. Her wooden platters and dishes were spotless. And the furniture! She had chairs with real backs, a table, and a big chest filled with clothes. There was one bureau that had cost forty-five dollars! Abe ran his finger over the shining dark wood. Sarah hung a small mirror above it, and he gasped when he looked at his reflection. This was the first looking glass that he had ever seen.

Most remarkable of all were the feather beds. One was laid on the pole bed, downstairs. Another was placed on a clean bearskin in the opposite corner to provide a sleeping place for the girls. The third was carried to the loft for the three boys. When Abe went to bed that night, he sank down gratefully into the comfortable feathers. The homespun blanket that covered him was soft and warm.

On either side, Dennis and Johnny were asleep. Abe lay between them, wide awake, staring into the darkness. The new Mrs. Lincoln was good and kind. He knew that. She had seemed pleased when Sally called her "Mamma." Somehow he couldn't. There was still a lonesome place in his heart for his own mother.

Something else was worrying him. Before going to bed, Sarah Lincoln had looked at him and Sally out of her calm gray eyes. "Tomorrow I aim to make you young ones look more human," she said. Abe wondered what she meant.

He found out the next morning. Tom and Dennis left early to go hunting. Abe went out to chop wood for the fireplace. When he came back, he met the three girls going down the path. Sally was walking between her two stepsisters, but what a different Sally! She wore a neat, pretty dress that had belonged to

Betsy. She had on Sarah's shawl. Her hair was combed in two neat pigtails. Her face had a clean, scrubbed look. Her eyes were sparkling. She was taking Betsy and Matilda to call on one of the neighbors.

"Good-bye, Mamma," she called.

Sarah stood in the doorway, waving to the girls. Then she saw Abe, his arms piled high with wood. "Come in," she said. "Sally has had her bath. Now I've got a tub of good hot water and a gourdful of soap waiting for you. Skedaddle out of those old clothes and throw them in the fire."

"I ain't got any others." Abe looked terrified.

"I don't aim to pluck your feathers without giving you some new ones." Sarah laughed. "I sat up late last night cutting down a pair of Mr. Johnston's old pants. I got a shirt, too, laid out here on the bed."

Slowly Abe started taking off his shirt. He looked fearfully at the tub of hot water.

"There's no call to be scared," said Sarah. "That tub won't bite. Now I'm going down to the spring. By the time I get back, I want you to have yourself scrubbed all over."

Abe stuck one toe into the water. He said, "Ouch!" and drew it out. He then tried again, and put in his whole foot. He put in his other foot. He sat down in the tub. By the time Sarah returned he was standing before the fire, dressed in the cut-down trousers and shirt of the late Mr. Johnston.

Sarah seemed pleased. "You look like a different boy," she said. "Those trousers are a mite too big, but you'll soon grow into them."

Abe was surprised how good it felt to be clean again. "Thank you, ma'am. Now I'd better get in some more wood."

"We have plenty of wood," said Sarah. "You see that stool? You sit down and let me get at your hair. It looks like a heap of underbrush."

Abe watched anxiously when she opened the top drawer of the bureau and took out a haw comb and a pair of scissors. I'll stand for it this time, he thought, because she's been so good to us. But if she pulls too hard —

Mrs. Lincoln *did* pull. But when Abe said "Ouch!" she patted his shoulder and waited a moment. He closed his eyes and screwed up his face, but he said nothing more. Perhaps she couldn't help pulling, he decided. Lock after lock she snipped off. He began to wonder if he was going to have any hair left by the time she got through.

"I've been watching you, Abe. You're a right smart

boy," she said. "Had much schooling?"

"I've just been to school by littles."

"Have you a mind to go again?"

"There ain't any school since Master Crawford left. Anyhow, Pappy doesn't set much store by eddication."

"What do you mean, Abe?"

"He says I know how to read and write and cipher and that's enough for anyone."

"You can read?" she asked.

"Yes'm, but I haven't any books."

"You can read and you haven't any books. I have books and I can't read."

Abe looked at her, amazed. "You have *books?*"

Sarah nodded, but said nothing more until she had finished cutting his hair. Then she led him over to the bureau.

"Now see if you don't like yourself better without that brush heap on top of your head," she asked him.

A boy with short neat hair gazed back at Abe from the mirror.

"I still ain't the prettiest boy in Pigeon Creek," he drawled, "but there ain't quite so much left to be ugly. I'm right glad, ma'am, you cleared away the brush heap."

Was he joking? He looked so solemn that Sarah could not be sure. Then he grinned. It was the first time that she had seen him smile.

"You're a caution, Abe," she said. "Now sit yourself down over there at the table, and I'll show you my books."

She opened the top drawer of the bureau and took out four worn little volumes. Although she could not read, she knew the titles. "Here they are: *Robinson Crusoe, Pilgrim's Progress, Sinbad the Sailor,* and *Aesop's Fables.*"

"Oh, ma'am, this book by Mr. Aesop is one the schoolmaster had. The stories are all about some smart talking animals."

He seemed to have forgotten her, as he bent his neat shorn head down over the pages. He chuckled when he read something that amused him. Sarah watched him curiously. He was not like her John. He was not like any boy that she had ever known. But the hungry look in his eyes went straight to her heart.

He looked up at her shyly. "Ma'am," he said, "will you let me read these books sometimes?"

"Why, Abe, you can read them any time you like. I'm giving them to you to keep."

"Oh, *Mamma!*" The name slipped out as though he were used to saying it. He had a feeling that Nancy, his own mother, had never gone away.

"You're my boy, now," Sarah told him, "and I aim to help you all I can. The next time a school keeps in these parts, I'm going to ask your pappy to let you and the other children go."

"Thank you, ma'am," said Abe. "I mean — thank you, Mamma."

CHAPTER *SIX*

Many changes were taking place in the Lincoln cabin. Sarah persuaded Tom to cut two holes in the walls for windows, and she covered them with greased paper to let in the light. He made a wooden door that could be shut against the cold winter winds. Abe and Dennis gave the walls and low ceiling a coat of whitewash, and Sarah spread her bright rag rugs on the new wooden floor.

"Aunt Sairy," Dennis told her, "you're some punkins. One just naturally has to be somebody when you're around."

Abe smiled up at her shyly. "It is sort of like the magic in that story of Sinbad you gave me."

The other children were asleep. Abe sprawled on the floor, making marks on a wooden shovel with a pointed stick. Tom, seated in one of his wife's chairs, was dozing on one side of the fireplace.

Sarah put down her knitting and looked around the cabin. "The place does look right cozy," she replied. "What is that you're doing, Abe?"

"Working my sums."

Tom opened his eyes. "You know how to figure enough already. Put that shovel up and go to bed."

Abe took a knife and scraped the figures from the wooden shovel. He placed it against one side of the fireplace. "Good night, Mamma," he said.

"Good night, Abe."

Sarah's eyes were troubled. She waited until Dennis had joined Abe in the loft, then turned to her husband. "I've been meaning to tell you, Tom, what a good pa you've been to my young ones."

She saw that he was pleased. "I've tried to be a good mother to Abe and Sally, too," she went on.

"You have been, Sairy. They took to you right off."

"I'm right glad, but there's something else I want to talk to you about, Tom." He was nodding again in his chair, and she paused to make sure that he was listening. "Abe's a smart boy. I told him the next time

39

a school keeps in these parts, I'd ask you to let him and the other children go."

"Humph!" Tom grunted. "There ain't any school for him to go to. Anyway, he wastes enough time as 'tis. He's always got his nose buried in those books you brought."

"That bothers me, too. I saw you cuff him the other day because he was reading."

"I had to, Sairy. I told him to come out and chop some wood, but he up and laughed in my face."

"He wasn't laughing at you, Tom. He was laughing at Sinbad."

"Who in tarnation is Sinbad?"

"A fellow in one of his books. Abe said that Sinbad sailed his flatboat up to a rock, and the rock was magnetized and pulled all the nails out of his boat. Then Sinbad fell into the water."

"That's what I mean," Tom exploded. "Dennis told him that book was most likely lies, but Abe keeps on reading it. Where is all this book learning going to get him? More'n I ever had."

"Maybe the Lord meant for young ones to be smarter than their parents," said Sarah, "or the world might never get any better."

Tom shook his head in dismay. "Women and their

fool notions! If I don't watch out, you'll be spoiling the boy more'n his own mammy did."

Sarah's cheeks were red as she bent over her knitting. Tom was right about one thing; there was no school for Abe to go to. But someday there would be. Every few weeks another clearing was made in the forest, and the neighbors gathered for a "house raising" to help put up a cabin. Then smoke would rise from a new chimney, and another new home would be started in the wilderness.

With so many new settlers, there was usually plenty of work for Abe. Whenever Tom did not need him at home, he hired out at twenty-five cents a day. He gave this money to his father. That was the law, Tom said. Not until Abe was twenty-one would he be allowed to keep his wages for himself. As a hired boy, he plowed corn, chopped wood, and did all kinds of chores. He did not like farming, but he managed to have fun.

"Pa taught me to work," Abe told one farmer who had hired him, "but he never taught me to love it."

The farmer scratched his head. He couldn't understand a boy who was always reading, and if Abe wasn't reading he was telling jokes. The farmer thought that Abe was lazy.

"Sometimes," the farmer said, "I get awful mad at

41

you, Abe Lincoln. You crack your jokes and spin your yarns, if you want to, while the men are eating their dinner. But don't you keep them from working."

The other farm hands liked to gather around Abe when they stopped to eat their noon meal. Sometimes he would stand on a tree stump and "speechify." The men would become so interested that they would be late getting back to the fields. Other times he would tell them stories that he had read in books or that he had heard from some traveler who had passed through Pigeon Creek. He nearly always had a funny story to tell.

Yet there was "something peculiarsome about Abe," as Dennis Hanks once said. He would be laughing one minute; the next minute he would look solemn and sad. He would walk along the narrow forest trails, a faraway look in his eyes. Someone would say "Howdy, Abe." Then he would grin and start cracking jokes again.

Although he worked such long hours, Abe still found time to read. He sat up late and got up early in the morning, and Sarah made the children keep quiet when he wanted to study. Sometimes he took a book to work with him. Instead of talking to the other farm hands at noon, he'd go off by himself and read a few

pages while he ate his dinner. People for miles around loaned him books. Sometimes he walked fifteen miles to Rockport, the county seat, to borrow books from John Pitcher, the town lawyer.

"Everything I want to know is in books," he told Dennis. "My best friend is a man who can give me a book I ain't read."

Late one afternoon, about two years after Sarah had arrived, Abe came home with a new book under his arm. Tom and Dennis had joined several of their neighbors in a big bear hunt and planned to be gone for several days. Abe planned to read — and read — and read.

"What do you think, Mamma?" he asked. "I have a chance to read the Declaration of Independence."

Sarah smiled into his eager eyes. "Now isn't that nice?"

He showed her the book. It belonged to David Turnham, the constable. Mr. Turnham had said that Abe might borrow it for several days, if he promised to be careful.

"What is it about?" Sarah asked.

"It has the laws of Indiana in it, and it tells how the government of our country was started." Abe's voice took on a new tone of excitement. "It has the Declaration of Independence in it and the Constitution, too."

He pulled a stool up to the fire and began to read. There was no sound in the little cabin except the steady click-click of Sarah's knitting needles. She glanced at him now and then. This tall, awkward boy had become very dear to her. As dear as her own children, perhaps even dearer, but he was harder to understand. No matter how much he learned, he wanted to learn more. He was always hungry — hungry for knowledge, not for bacon and corn bread the way Johnny was. The idea made her chuckle.

Abe did not hear. He laid the book on his knee and stared into the flames. His lips were moving, although he made no sound.

"What are you saying to yourself?" Sarah asked. "You look so far away."

"Why, Mamma." Abe looked up with a start. "I was just recollecting some of the words out of the Declaration of Independence. It says all men are created equal."

"You don't mean to tell me!" Sarah was pleased because Abe was.

"I'm going to learn as much of the Declaration as I can by heart, before I take the book back," he said. "That way I can always keep the words."

"I declare," said Sarah, "you grow new ideas inside your head as fast as you add inches on top of it."

CHAPTER *SEVEN*

A BE WENT RIGHT ON adding inches. By the time he was fourteen he was as tall as his father. Sally was working as a hired girl that summer for Mr. and Mrs. Josiah Crawford. Abe worked for them off and on. One afternoon he finished his chores early, and Mrs. Crawford sent him home. Abe was glad. Josiah had lent him a new book — a life of George Washington — and he wanted to start reading it.

When he reached the Lincoln cabin, he found Betsy and Mathilda waiting outside for their mother. She stood before the mirror in the cabin, putting on her sunbonnet.

"Your pa and Dennis have gone squirrel hunting,"

she said, as she tied the strings in a neat bow beneath her chin. "The gals and I are going to visit a new neighbor. Will you keep an eye on Johnny and put some 'taters on to boil for supper?"

"Oh Ma, not potatoes again?"

"They will be right tasty with a mess of squirrel. Before you put the 'taters on — "

Abe patted the book inside his shirt front. "I can read?" he asked.

"You can, after you go down to the horse trough and wash your head."

"Wash my head? How come?" Abe wailed.

"Take a look at that ceiling, and you'll know how come. See that dark spot? Your head made that. You're getting so tall you bump into the ceiling every time you climb into the loft."

Abe rolled his eyes upward. "If some of that learning I've got cooped up in my head starts leaking out, how can I help it?"

Sarah refused to be put off by any of his foolishness. "When you track dirt into the house, I can wash the floor," she said. "But I can't get to the ceiling so easy. It needs a new coat of whitewash, but there's no use in doing it if your head ain't clean.

"All right," said Abe meekly.

"Take a gourdful of soap with you," said Sarah. "And mind you, no reading until you finish washing your hair."

He grumbled under his breath as he walked down to the horse trough. With a new book waiting to be read, washing his hair seemed a waste of time. But if that was what Sarah wanted, he would do it. He lathered his head with soap and ducked it into the water. Some of the soap got into his eyes, and he began to sputter. He heard a giggle.

"Hey, Johnny, is that you?" he said. "Get a bucket of water—quick!"

Johnny, the eight-year-old stepbrother, was glad to oblige. He poured bucket after bucket of water over Abe's head. Finally all of the soap was rinsed out of his hair. Abe took the tail of his shirt and wiped the soap out of his eyes. Both boys were covered with water. The ground around the horse trough was like a muddy little swamp. Johnny was delighted. He liked to feel the mud squish up between his toes.

"Look at me, Abe," he shouted. "Ain't we having fun?"

Abe took his young stepbrother by the hand. His eyes were twinkling. "I've thought of something else that's fun. Come on, we're going to play a joke on Mamma."

When Sarah returned to the cabin late that afternoon, she noticed that Abe's hair was still damp. He was very quiet as he stood by the fireplace and swung the big kettle outward. He dipped out the potatoes with an iron spoon. Tom and Dennis came in, both somewhat grumpy. They had not brought back a single squirrel.

Only Johnny seemed in good spirits. He whispered in Mathilda's ear. They both began to giggle. By the time the family had gathered around the table, Betsy and Dennis had been let in on the secret, whatever it was. They were red in the face from trying not to laugh.

"Quiet!" said Tom. "Quiet, while I say the blessing."

"We thank thee, Lord — " he began.

Tom usually gave thanks for each kind of food on the table. But today there was only a dish of dried-up potatoes. "We thank thee, Lord," he went on, "for all these blessings."

"Mighty poor blessings," said Abe.

The girls giggled again. Dennis threw back his head and roared. Johnny was laughing so hard that he fell off his stool. He lay on the floor, rolling and shrieking.

"I wish you young ones would stop carrying on," said Sarah, "and tell me what you're carrying on about."

"Oh, Mamma, can't you see?" said Betsy. "Look up."

Sarah gasped. Marching across the cabin ceiling were the muddy marks of two bare feet.

"Don't they look like Johnny's feet?" Mathilda asked.

"Johnny Johnston, you come right here," said Sarah sternly.

Johnny picked himself up from the rag rug before the fireplace. He went over and stood before his mother. His blue eyes danced. This was one scolding that he looked forward to.

"Now tell me the truth. What do you mean by — "

Sarah paused. She could hardly scold her son for walking on the ceiling.

Johnny had been told exactly what to say. "I got my feet all muddy down at the horse trough," he explained. "Then I walked on the ceiling."

"You walked on the ceiling? Johnny Johnston, you know it's wicked to lie."

"I'm not lying. Those are my footprints."

Sarah looked again. The footprints were too small to belong to anyone but Johnny. She looked at Abe.

He seemed to have taken a sudden liking for boiled potatoes, and kept his eyes on his plate.

"Abe Lincoln, is this some of your tomfoolery?"

"I — I reckon so."

"But how —"

"It was easy," Johnny interrupted. "I held my legs stiff and Abe held me upside down, and I walked."

Abe stood up, pushing back his stool. He glanced toward the door.

Sarah was not often angry. When she was, she reminded her children of a mother hen ruffling its feathers. "Well, Abe, have you got anything to say for yourself?"

Abe shook his head. Suddenly his joke did not seem quite so funny.

"I declare!" said Sarah. "A big boy like you! You ought to be spanked."

The children looked at tall, lanky Abe towering over their mother. They burst out laughing again. "Mamma's going to spank Abe!" they chanted. "Mamma's going to spank Abe."

Dennis brought both hands down on the table with a loud whack. "That's a good one, that is," he roared.

Sarah threw her apron over her head. The children watched the peculiar way the apron began to shake. When she took it down, they saw that she was laughing. She was laughing so hard that the tears ran down her cheeks.

"I reckon I'll have to let you off, Abe," she said. "You'd be a mite too big for me to handle."

Tom jumped up. "He ain't too big for me. He ain't too big for a good-sized hickory switch."

Sarah bit her lip, her own brief anger forgotten. "Now, Tom," she protested.

"You ain't going to talk me out of it this time."

" — I was aiming to whitewash the ceiling, Pa," said Abe. "Ma said it needed a fresh coat."

Sarah looked relieved. "That is exactly what he can do. Whitewash the ceiling."

"He can after I've given him a licking."

Sarah put out her hand. "Sit down, Tom, and finish

your 'taters before they get cold. I figure it this way.
Before Abe starts reading that new book, he can
whitewash the ceiling. The walls, too. That ought to
learn him not to cut up any more didos."

Sarah pulled down her mouth, trying to look stern.
Tom sat down and started to eat his potato.

"You're a good one, Sairy," he chuckled. "You sure
know how to get work out of him."

Abe looked at her gratefully. At the same time he
was disappointed. He had been thinking about that
book all afternoon.

The next morning Sarah shooed everyone out of the
cabin. Abe was down by the horse trough, mixing the
whitewash in a big tub. By the time he returned, she
had a bucket of hot water and a gourdful of soft soap
ready. After washing the inside of the cabin he got
busy with the whitewash. First he did the walls. Then
he did the rafters and the ceiling. He cocked his head,
gazing at the muddy footprints.

"They make a right pretty picture, ma'am. Shall I
leave them on for decoration?"

Sarah, seated on a stool by the fireplace, looked up
from her sewing. "Abe, you big scamp. You get that
ceiling nice and white, or I'll be carrying out my
threat."

The corners of her mouth were twitching. Abe grinned, glad to be at peace with her again.

"After I finish here," he asked, "do you have any more chores?"

"No, Abe. I reckon there will be time for you to do some reading. But first, you finish your whitewashing. Then there's something I want to talk to you about."

Abe dipped his brush into the whitewash again and again, until he had covered up the last telltale mark of Johnny's feet. The cabin was bright and shining when he finished. He pulled another stool up to the fireplace and sat facing Sarah.

"I wasn't meaning to tell you just yet," she said. "Leastways until I had a chance to talk to your pa."

"What is it, Mamma?"

"There's a new neighbor come to Pigeon Creek," she said. "Man by the name of James Swaney. He is farming now, but he is fixing to keep a school next winter."

Abe jumped up and stood looking down at her. "Do you reckon that Pa — "

"Your pa is worried," Sarah interrupted. "Money-worried. He may have to sell some of his land. That's why he gets riled so easy — like yesterday."

Abe flushed.

"I want you to be careful," said Sarah. "Try not to get his dander up."

"I'll try not to."

"Maybe you recollect what I promised you when I first came. I said I'd ask your pa to let you go to school again. Now I'm a body that believes in keeping my promises. I just want to wait till he feels good."

Sarah's sewing basket spilled to the floor, as Abe pulled her to her feet. He put his long arms around her waist and gave her a good bear hug.

"Abe Lincoln, you're most choking me," she said breathlessly. "Here I was thinking how grown up you were getting to be. Now you be acting like a young one again."

Abe kissed her on the cheek.

CHAPTER *EIGHT*

ABE SAT UP LATE, holding his book close to the flickering flames in the fireplace. As the rain drummed on the roof, his thoughts were far away. He was with General Washington in a small boat crossing the Delaware River on a cold Christmas night many years before. He was fighting the Battle of Trenton with a handful of brave American soldiers. They must have wanted very much to be free, he decided, to be willing to fight so hard and suffer so much.

"Isn't it getting too dark for you to see?" Sarah called sleepily.

"Yes, Mamma."

Carefully Abe placed the precious little volume between two logs in the wall of the cabin. This was his bookcase. As he climbed into the loft, he wondered if the book told about the time George Washington became President. He would have to wait until morning to find out.

He was up early. But his face grew pale when he reached for the book. During the night the rain had leaked in on it through a crack in the logs. The pages were wet and stuck together. The binding was warped. Sally was starting down the path toward the Crawford cabin when Abe called after her.

"Wait! I'm coming with you."

He thrust the book inside his buckskin shirt. Sally tried to comfort him, but Abe kept wondering what Mr. Crawford was going to say. He was a little scared of Josiah. Some of the boys called him "Old Bluenose" because of the large purple vein on the side of his nose. It made him look rather cross. He probably would want Abe to pay for the book, and Abe had no money.

He opened the Crawford gate and marched up to the kitchen door. Josiah, his wife Elizabeth, and Sammy, their little boy, were having breakfast. When Abe explained what had happened, Mrs. Crawford patted his shoulder. He liked her. She was always nice to him, but he knew that her husband was the one who would decide about the book. Josiah took it in his big hands and looked at the stained pages.

"Well, Abe," he said slowly, "I won't be hard on you. If you want to pull fodder three days for me, that ought to pay for the book."

"Starting right now?"

"Yep, starting right now," Josiah was actually smiling. "Then you can have the book to keep."

Abe caught his breath. What a lucky boy he was! Three days' work and he could keep the book! He would have a chance to read about George Washington any time he wanted to.

Never had he worked harder or faster than he did that morning. When the noon dinner bell rang, he seemed to be walking on air as he followed Josiah into the cabin. Sally was putting dinner on the table. Abe slipped up behind her and pulled one of her pigtails. Taken by surprise, she jumped and dropped a pitcher of cream. The pitcher did not break, but the cream spilled and spread over the kitchen floor.

"Abe Lincoln! Look what you made me do!" cried Sally. "I just washed that floor. And look at that good cream going to waste."

" 'Tain't going to waste." Abe pointed to Elizabeth Crawford's cat, which was lapping up the delicious

yellow stream. Then he began to sing: "Cat's in the cream jar, shoo, shoo, shoo!"

"Stop trying to show off!" said Sally.

She was angry, but Sammy, Elizabeth's little boy, shouted with delight. That was all the encouragement Abe needed. The fact that he could not carry a tune did not seem to bother him.

Cat's in the cream jar, shoo, shoo, shoo!
Cat's in the cream jar, shoo, shoo, shoo!
Skip to my Lou, my darling.

Sally was down on her hands and knees, wiping up the cream. "Stop singing that silly song and help me."

Instead, Abe danced a jig. He leaned down and pulled her other pigtail.

" 'Sally's in the cream jar, shoo, shoo, shoo.' "

"That's enough, Abe," said Elizabeth Crawford.

" 'Skip to my Lou, my darling.' " He whirled around on his bare feet and made a sweeping bow. Sally was close to tears.

"Abe, I told you to stop," said Elizabeth Crawford. "You ought to be ashamed, teasing your sister. If you keep on acting that way, what do you think is going to become of you?

"Me?" Abe drew himself up. "What's going to become of me? I'm going to be President."

Elizabeth looked at him, a lanky barefoot boy with trousers too short. His shirt was in rags. His black hair was tousled. She sank into a chair, shaking with laughter. "A pretty President you'd make, now wouldn't you?"

She had no sooner spoken than she wanted to take back the words. All of the joy went out of his face. Sally was too angry to notice.

"Maybe you're going to be President," she said. "But first you'd better learn to behave."

"I — I was just funning, Sally."

Something in his voice made Sally look up. She saw the hurt expression in his eyes. "I know you were," she said hastily. "I'm not mad any more."

Abe ate his dinner in silence. He did not seem to be the same boy who had been cutting up only a few minutes before. Elizabeth kept telling herself that she should not have laughed at him. He did try to show off sometimes. But he was a good boy. She thought more of him than of any of the other young folks in Pigeon Creek. Not for anything would she have hurt his feelings. When he pushed back his stool, she followed him out into the yard.

"About your being President," she said. "I wasn't aiming to make fun of you. I just meant that you — with all your tricks and jokes — "

"I reckon I know what you meant," said Abe quietly. "All the same, Mrs. Crawford, I don't always mean to delve and grub and such like."

There was a look of determination on his face that she had not seen before. "I think a heap of you," she went on, "and I don't want to see you disappointed. It's a fine thing to be ambitious. But don't let reading about George Washington give you notions that can't come to anything."

Abe threw back his shoulders. "I aim to study and get ready, and then the chance will come."

He lifted his battered straw hat and started down the path toward the field. He walked with dignity. Elizabeth had not realized that he was so tall.

"I declare," she said, "he really means it!"

Sammy had come up and heard her. "Means what, Mamma?" he asked.

Elizabeth took his hand. "Didn't you know, Sammy? Abe is fixing to be President someday."

CHAPTER *NINE*

On SUNDAY MORNING the Lincolns went to church.
All except Sarah; she had a headache.

"I'll go, Ma," said Abe. "When I come back, I'll tell
you what the preacher said."

Sarah smiled at him fondly. Abe could listen to a
sermon, then come home and repeat it almost word
for word. "I'd rather hear you preachify," she said,
"than the preacher himself."

Tom and his family walked single file into the log
meetinghouse and took their places on one of the long
wooden benches. John Carter, sitting on the bench in
front of them, turned and nodded. Carter had promised to buy the Lincolns' south field. He would have
the papers ready for Tom to sign on Monday. Tom

needed the money, but the very thought of selling any
of his land made him grumpy. He twisted and turned
on the hard wooden bench during the long sermon.
He hardly heard a word that the preacher was saying.

Abe leaned forward and listened eagerly. The
preacher was a tall, thin man. He flung his arms about.
His voice grew louder and hoarser as the morning
passed. He paused only to catch his breath, or when
the members of the congregation shouted, "Amen."
After the final hymn, he stood at the door shaking
hands.

"Brother Lincoln," he said, "I want you to meet up with a new neighbor. This here is Mr. Swaney."

Tom shook hands. Then the preacher introduced Abe.

"Are you the new schoolmaster?" Abe asked.

"I don't figure on starting school till after harvest," Mr. Swaney replied. "Will you be one of my scholars?"

"I'd sure like to come." Abe glanced at his father.

"I reckon not," said Tom stiffly. "Abe has had as much schooling as he needs."

Back at the cabin, Sarah had dinner on the table. Tom cheered up as he and Dennis started "swapping yarns." Both were good storytellers, and each tried to tell a better story than the other.

Abe did not like being left out of the conversation. "Pa," he asked, "can you answer me a question about something in the Bible?"

"I figure I can answer any question you got sense enough to ask."

Johnny and Mathilda nudged each other. They knew what was coming. One day when the preacher stopped by, Abe had asked him the same question. The preacher had been downright flustered when he couldn't answer.

"It's just this, Pa," Abe went on. "Who was the father of Zebedee's children?"

Tom flushed. "Any uppity young one can ask a question. But can he answer it? Suppose *you* tell *me* who was the father of Zebedee's children?"

"I sort of figured," said Abe, "that Zebedee was."

Everyone was laughing except Tom; then he laughed, too. Sarah was glad. Abe had told her that Mr. Swaney was at church. She was going to talk to her husband that afternoon about sending the children to school, and she wanted him to be in a good humor.

"What did the preacher have to say?" she asked.

"Well — " Tom was trying to remember. "What he said sort of got lost in the way he was saying it. How some of those preachers do hop and skip about!"

"I like to hear a preacher who acts like he's fighting bees," said Abe.

Sarah nodded. The description fitted the preacher "like his own moccasin," she said.

"You menfolks wait outside," she added. "Soon as the gals and I get the dishes done, we'll be out to hear Abe preachify."

The afternoon was warm. Sarah fanned herself with her apron as she sat down at one end of a fallen log near the door. The rest of the family lined up beside her. Abe stood before them, his arms folded, as he repeated the sermon he had heard that morning. Now and then he paused and shook his finger in the faces of his congregation. He pounded with one fist on the palm of his other hand.

"Brethren and sisters," said Abe, "there ain't no chore too big for the Lord, no chore too small. The Good Book says He knows when a sparrow falls. Yet He had time to turn this great big wilderness into this here land where we have our homes. Just think, folks, this Pigeon Creek had no one but Indians living here a few years back. And today we got cabins with smoke coming out of the chimneys. We got crops agrowing. We got a meetinghouse where we can come together and praise the Lord — "

Abe paused.

"Amen!" said Tom.

"Amen!" said the others.

"Don't forget," Abe went on, "all of this was the Lord's doing. Let us praise Him for His goodness."

He reached down, plucked a fistful of grass, and mopped his forehead. In much the same way had the preacher used his bandanna handkerchief. The Lincoln family rose, sang "Praise God from Whom All Blessings Flow," and church was over.

The young folks drifted away. Tom stretched out on the grass for his Sunday afternoon nap.

"Abe tells me that new Mr. Swaney was at church," Sarah said.

Tom opened his eyes. Before he had a chance to go back to sleep, she spoke again.

"He's fixing to keep a school next winter."

"So I hear," said Tom cautiously.

"He charges seventy-five cents for each scholar. Some schoolmasters charge a dollar."

"Sounds like a lot of money."

"Several of the neighbors are fixing to send their young ones," Sarah went on. "Mr. Swaney doesn't ask for cash money. He'll take skins or farm truck. We can manage that, I reckon."

Tom yawned. "Plumb foolishness, if you ask me. But Johnny and Mathilda are your young ones. If you want to send them — "

"I want Sally and Abe to go, too," Sarah interrupted. "Abe most of all. He is the one school will do the most good. He's the one who wants it most."

Tom sat up. "I can spare the younger ones, but I need Abe. With us poorer than Job's turkey, you ought to know that."

Sarah listened patiently. "I ain't talking about right now. Mr. Swaney won't start his school till winter. Farm work will be slack then."

"I can hire Abe out to split rails, even in cold weather," Tom reminded her. "Maybe I can get some odd jobs as a carpenter, and Abe can help me."

"Abe ain't no great hand at carpentry."

"He can learn. Why, he's fourteen, Sairy. The idea, a big strapping boy like that going to school. I tell you, I won't have it."

"But I promised him."

It was the first time that Tom had ever heard a

quaver in his wife's voice. He looked away uneasily. "If you made a promise you can't keep, that's your lookout. You might as well stop nagging me, Sairy. My mind is made up."

To make sure that there would be no more conversation on the subject, he got up and stalked across the grass. He lay down under another tree, out of hearing distance. Sarah sat on the log for a long time. Abe came back and sat down beside her. He could tell, by looking at her, that she had been talking to his father about letting him go to school. He knew, without asking any questions, that his father had said no.

Sarah laid her hand on his knee. "Your pa is a good man," she said loyally. "Maybe he will change his mind."

CHAPTER *TEN*

Hurry up and eat your breakfast, Abe," said Tom
the next morning. "We're going to cut corn for that
skinflint, John Carter."

Sarah passed her husband a plate of hot corn bread.
"Why, Tom, it ain't fitting to talk that way about a
neighbor. Before the children, too."

Tom poured a generous helping of sorghum mo-
lasses over his bread. "I'm an honest man. It's fitting
that I call Carter what he is, and he's a skinflint. He
is only paying Abe and me ten cents a day."

"Other folks pay you two bits."

"I ain't got any other work right now. Carter knows
I need all the money I can lay my hands on. The way
he beat me down on the price for my south field."

71

"I wish you didn't have to sell." -

"Wishing won't do any good. I need cash money mighty bad. Remember, this farm ain't paid for yet."

He got up and walked over to the chest. He picked up the sharp knife he used for cutting corn. "Get your knife, Abe, and come along."

Abe walked behind his father along the path through the woods. "That Mr. Swaney was right nice," he said.

Tom grunted.

"He is waiting to start his school until after harvest," Abe went on. "Nat Grigsby is going. Allen Gentry is going, and he is two years older than me."

"Allen's pa is a rich man," said Tom gruffly. "Maybe he's got money to burn, but poor folks like us have to earn our keep."

"But Pa — "

"I declare, your tongue is loose at both ends today. Can't you stop plaguing me? First your ma, then you. You ought to see I'm worried."

Abe said nothing more. He pulled a book out of the front of his shirt and began to read as he strode along the path. Tom looked back over his shoulder.

"Don't let John Carter catch you with that book."

"I brought it along so I can read while I eat my dinner. I'll put it away before we get to the Carter place."

"Eddication!" said Tom in disgust. "I never had any, and I get along better'n if I had. Take figuring. If a fellows owes me money, I take a burnt stick and make a mark on the wall. When he pays me, I take a dishrag and wipe the mark off. That's better than getting all hot and bothered trying to figure.

"And writing? I can write my name, and that's all the writing I need. But the most tomfoolery of all is reading. You don't see *me* waste *my* time reading any books."

The path ended at the edge of the woods, and Tom opened the gate into the Carter cornfield. Row after row of tall corn stretched away in even, straight lines. Mr. Carter was waiting.

"Ready to sign over that south field, Tom?" he asked. "A lawyer from Rockport is drawing up the papers. He is riding up with them this morning. I'll see you at dinnertime."

After John Carter had gone back to his cabin, Tom and Abe set to work. Using their sharp knives, they began cutting the corn close to the ground. They stood the tall golden stalks on end, tying them together in neat shocks or bundles. By the time the sun stood directly overhead, several long rows had been cut and stacked, and John Carter was coming toward them across the field. It was noon.

Abe laid aside his knife, sat down on the rail fence, and pulled out his book. He took a piece of corn bread wrapped in a corn husk from his pocket. As he ate, he read, paying no attention to the conversation taking place a few feet away.

"Come and sit down, Tom," said Carter.

Tom sat on a tree stump. Carter was being more friendly than usual. He was carrying a gourdful of ink, which he placed on another stump. He set down a deerskin bag, which jingled pleasantly with coins. In one pocket he found a turkey-buzzard pen. From another he brought out an official-looking paper.

"Here is the deed for the south field," he explained. "Here's a pen. I'll hold the ink for you. You make your mark right here."

"I don't need to make my mark," said Tom proudly. "I know how to sign my name."

"Then hurry up and do it. Mrs. Carter has dinner ready, and I got to get back to the house."

Tom took the paper and looked at it uncertainly. "I don't sign any paper till I know what I'm signing. I want time to — to go over this careful like."

He could make out a few of the words, and that was all. But not for anything would he admit that he could not read it.

"You told me you wanted to sell," said Carter. "I said I would buy. I am keeping my part of the bargain. I even brought the money with me."

Tom's face grew red. He looked down at the paper in his hand. He glanced at Abe seated on the fence. A struggle was taking place between pride and common sense. Common sense won.

"Abe, come here," he called.

Abe went on reading.

Tom raised his voice. "Abe! When I tell you to come, I mean for you to come."

The boy looked up from his book with a start. "Yes, Pa. Did you want me?"

"Hustle over here and look at this paper. Carter is in a mighty big hurry for me to sign something I ain't had a chance to read."

"You have had plenty of time to read it," said Carter. "But if you don't want to sell, I can call the whole deal off."

Abe reached out a long arm and took the paper. He read it slowly. "Pa," he asked, "don't you aim to sell Mr. Carter just the south field?"

"You know I'm selling him just the south field," said Tom.

"Then don't sign this."

Carter picked up the moneybag clanking with coins. He tossed it into the air and caught it neatly. Tom looked at it. He wanted that money! He looked at Abe.

"Why shouldn't I sign?" he asked.

"If you do, you'll be selling Mr. Carter most of your farm."

John Carter was furious. "Don't try to tell me a country jake like you can read! That paper says the south field, as plain as the nose on your face."

"It says that and a sight more, Mr. Carter," Abe drawled. "It says the north field, too. It says the east and the west fields. There wouldn't be much farm left for Pa, except the part our cabin is setting on."

A dispute between men in Pigeon Creek usually ended in a fight. Tom Lincoln doubled up his fists. "Put them up, Carter."

The two men rolled over and over in a confused tangle of arms and legs. Now Tom Lincoln was on top. Now it was John Carter. "Go it, Pa," Abe shouted from the fence. "Don't let that old skinflint get you down." After a few minutes, Carter lay on his back gasping for breath.

" 'Nuff!" he cried. Tom let him scramble to his feet.

Carter began brushing himself off. "It ain't fitting to fight a neighbor," he whined, "just because of a mistake."

"Mistake nothing!" Tom snorted. "Somebody lied, and it wasn't Abe."

"I'll have a new paper made out, if you like," said Carter.

Tom looked at him with scorn. "You ain't got enough money to buy my south field. But I'll thank you for the ten cents you owe us. Abe and I each did a half day's work."

Tom's right eye was swelling, and by the time he reached home it was closed. The bump on the side of his head was the size of a hen's egg. There was a long scratch down his cheek.

Sarah was kneeling before the fireplace, raking ashes over the potatoes that she had put in to bake. She jumped up in alarm.

"What's the matter? What happened?" she asked.

"It was like Pa said," Abe told her. "Mr. Carter is a skinflint."

Sarah took Tom by the arm and made him sit down on a stool. She touched the swollen eye with gentle fingers.

"It don't hurt much," he said.

"I reckon Mr. Carter hurts more," Abe spoke up again. "He has two black eyes."

Tom slapped his thigh and roared with laughter. "He sure does. But if it hadn't been for Abe — "

He stopped, embarrassed. Sarah was soaking a cloth in a basin of cold water. She laid it on his eye.

"What started it all?"

"You tell them, Abe," said Tom.

"That Mr. Carter ain't as smart as he thinks he is," Abe explained. "He had a paper for Pa to sign, and tried to make out it was for just the south field. And do you know what, Mamma? When Pa asked me to read it, why, it was for almost our whole farm."

"You don't mean to tell me!" said Sarah.

"Carter said he'd have a new paper made out. But I told him," Tom added with a touch of pride, "I could do without his money."

"Good for you!" Sarah said, beaming. "Don't you fret. We'll squeak through somehow. But what if you had signed that paper? The farm would have been sold right out from under us. I reckon we can feel mighty proud of Abe."

"Well," Tom admitted, "it didn't hurt that he knew how to read. When did you say Mr. Swaney aims to start his school?"

"Right after harvest," said Abe, before his step-mother had a chance to answer.

Tom ignored him and went on talking to his wife. "Now, mind you, Sairy, I ain't saying Abe needs any more eddication. I ain't saying it is fitting a son should know more'n his pa. But if you think the young ones should go to this new school for a spell, I won't say no."

He rose and stalked out of the cabin. Then he came back and stuck his head in at the door.

"Mind you, Abe, you forget to do your chores just one time, and that schoolmaster won't be seeing you again."

"Come back in and sit down, Tom," said Sarah. "Supper is nearly ready. Besides, Abe has something that needs saying."

Abe looked at his stepmother in surprise. Then he looked at his father. "I'm much obliged, Pa," he said.

CHAPTER *ELEVEN*

A̲FTER A FEW WEEKS at Master Swaney's school, Abe had to stop and go to work again. When he was seventeen, he had a chance to attend another school kept by Azel Dorsey. Nearly every Friday afternoon there were special exercises, and the scholars spoke pieces. For the final program on the last day of school, the boys had built a platform outside the log schoolhouse. Parents, brothers and sisters, and friends found seats on fallen logs and on the grass. They listened proudly as, one by one, the children came forward and each recited a poem or a speech.

Master Dorsey walked to the front of the platform. He held up his hand for silence. "Ladies and gentlemen," he said, "we come to the last number on our program. Twenty-five years ago Thomas Jefferson became President of these United States. We shall now hear the speech he made that day. Abraham Lincoln will recite it for us."

Sarah Lincoln, from under her pink sunbonnet, stole a glance at Tom. "I hope that Abe does well," she whispered.

Abe did do well. He forgot that he was growing too fast, that his hand were too big, and that his trousers were too short. For a few minutes he made his audience forget it. Master Dorsey seemed to swell with pride. "If that boy lives," he thought, "he is going to be a noted man someday." Elizabeth Crawford, sitting in the front row, remembered what he had said about being President. If she closed her eyes, she could almost imagine that Thomas Jefferson was speaking. When Abe finished and made an awkward bow, she joined in the hearty burst of applause.

"Do you know where he got that piece?" she asked her husband in a low voice. "From *The Kentucky Preceptor*, one of the books you loaned him. It makes a body feel good to think we helped him. Look at Mrs. Lincoln! She couldn't be more pleased if Abe was her own son."

Sarah waited to walk home with him. "I was mighty proud of you today," she said. "Why, what's the matter? You look mighty down-in-the-mouth for a boy who spoke his piece so well on the last day."

"I was thinking that this is the last day," he answered. "The last day I'll ever go to school, most likely."

"Well, you're seventeen now."

"Yes, I'm seventeen, and I ain't had a year's schooling all told. I can't even talk proper. I forget and say 'ain't' though I know it ain't — I mean isn't right."

"It seems to me you're educating yourself with all those books you read," said Sarah cheerfully.

"I've already read all the books for miles around. Besides, I want to see places. I can't help it, Ma, I want to get away."

Sarah looked at him fondly. She wished that she could find some way to help him.

Abe found ways to help himself. He was never to go to school again, but he could walk to Rockport to attend trials in the log courthouse. He liked to listen to the lawyers argue their cases. Sometimes he would write down what they said on a piece of paper. Now and then he had a chance to borrow a book that he had not read before from some new settler. He read the old books over and over again. He liked to read the newspapers to which Mr. Gentry, Allen's father, subscribed. The papers told what was going on in the big world outside of Pigeon Creek.

James Gentry owned the log store at the crossroads, where the little town, Gentryville, had grown up. His partner, William Jones, was one of Abe's best friends, and Abe spent nearly every evening at the store. It became the favorite meeting place for the men and boys who lived close by.

"Howdy, Abe!" Everyone seemed to be saying it at once when he came in.

"The Louisville paper came today," William Jones might add. "Here you are! The fellows have been waiting for you to holler out the news."

Abe sat on the counter, swinging his long legs, as he read the newspaper out loud. The men sat quietly, except when William got up to throw another log on the fire or to light another candle. Abe read on and on. After he finished the paper, they talked about what he had read. They argued about many things, from politics to religion. They always wanted to know what Abe thought. Many times they stayed until nearly midnight listening to him.

One evening, not long after Abe's nineteenth birthday, he walked home from the store in great excitement. He had been very sad since his sister Sally had
died in January, but tonight he seemed more cheerful.
Sarah looked up to find him standing in the doorway.

"What do you think has happened, Ma?" he asked.
"I am going to New Orleans."

"How come, Abe?"

Sarah knew that prosperous farmers sometimes
loaded their corn and other farm products on big flatboats. These flatboats were floated down the Ohio

and Mississippi rivers to New Orleans, where the cargoes were sold. But the Lincolns raised only enough for their own use. They never had anything left over to sell. Nor could they afford to build a flatboat for the long trip down the rivers.

"How come?" Sarah asked again.

Abe seized her around the waist and danced her across the floor. She was out of breath, but laughing, when he let her go.

"Allen Gentry is taking a cargo of farm truck down to New Orleans to sell," he explained. "His pa has hired me to help on the flatboat. Mr. Gentry will pay me eight dollars a month. I reckon Pa will be pleased about that."

Abe himself was pleased because he was going to see something of the world. New Orleans was seven hundred miles away. It was a big and important city. Sarah was pleased because this was the chance that Abe had been wanting.

He had grown so tall that she had to throw back her head to look up at him. "I'm right glad for you," she said.

CHAPTER *TWELVE*

To a boy brought up in the backwoods, the trip down the rivers was one long adventure. Abe sat at the forward oar, guiding the big flatboat through the calm, blue waters of the Ohio, while Allen cooked supper on deck. Afterward Abe told stories.

After they had reached the southern tip of Illinois, where the Ohio emptied into the yellow waters of the Mississippi, there was little time for stories. The boys never knew what to expect next. One minute the river would be quiet and calm, the next it would rise in the fury of a sudden storm. The waves rose in a yellow flood that poured over the deck. Allen at the back oar, Abe at the front oar, had a hard time keeping the big flatboat from turning over.

At the end of each day, the boys tied up the boat at some place along the shore. One night after they had gone to sleep, several robbers crept on board. Abe and Allen awoke just in time. After a long, hard fight, the robbers turned and fled.

These dangers only made their adventures seem more exciting. It was exciting, too, to be a part of the traffic of the river. They saw many other flatboats like their own. The biggest thrill was in watching the steamboats, with giant paddle wheels that turned the water into foam. Their decks were painted a gleaming white, and their brass rails shown in the sun. No wonder they were called "floating palaces," thought Abe. Sometimes passengers standing by the rail waved to the boys.

Each day of their journey brought gentler breezes, warmer weather. Cottonwood and magnolia trees grew on the low swampy banks of both shores. The boys passed cotton fields, where gangs of Negro slaves were at work. Some of them were singing as they bent to pick the snowy white balls of cotton. A snatch of song came floating over the water:

> Oh, brother, don't get weary,
> Oh, brother, don't get weary,

Oh, brother, don't get weary,
We're waiting for the Lord.

Abe leaned on his oar to listen. A few minutes later he pointed to a big house with tall white pillars in the middle of a beautiful garden.

"Nice little cabin those folks have," he said dryly. "Don't recollect seeing anything like that up in Pigeon Creek."

"Why, Abe, you haven't seen anything yet. Just wait till you get to New Orleans."

This was Allen's second trip, and he was eager to show Abe the sights. A few days later they were walking along the New Orleans waterfront. Ships from many different countries were tied up at the wharves. Negro slaves were rolling bales of cotton onto a steamboat. Other Negroes, toting huge baskets on their heads, passed by. Sailors from many lands, speaking strange tongues, rubbed elbows with fur trappers dressed in buckskins from the far Northwest. A cotton planter in a white suit glanced at the two youths from Pigeon Creek. He seemed amused. Abe looked down at his homespun blue jeans. He had not realized that all young men did not wear them.

"Reckon we do look different from some of the folks down here," he said, as he and Allen turned into a narrow street.

Here there were more people — always more people. The public square was crowded. Abe gazed in awe at the cathedral. This tall Spanish church, with its two graceful towers, was so different from the log meetinghouse that the Lincolns attended.

Nor was there anything back in Pigeon Creek like the tall plaster houses, faded by time and weather into warm tones of pink and lavender and yellow. The balconies, or porches, on the upper floors had wrought-iron railings of such delicate design that they looked like iron lace.

Once the boys paused before a wrought-iron gate. At the end of a long passageway they could see a courtyard where flowers bloomed and a fountain splashed in the sunshine. Abe turned to watch a handsome carriage roll by over the cobblestones. He looked down the street toward the river, which sheltered ships from all over the world.

"All this makes me feel a little like Sinbad," he said, "but I reckon even Sinbad never visited New Orleans. I sure do like it here."

But soon Abe began to see other sights that made him sick at heart. He and Allen passed a warehouse where slaves were being sold at auction. A crowd had gathered inside. Several Negroes were standing on a platform called an auction block. One by one they stepped forward. A man called an auctioneer asked in a loud voice, "What am I offered? Who will make the first bid?"

"Five hundred," called one man.

"Six hundred," called another.

The bids mounted higher. Each slave was sold to the

man who bid, or offered to pay, the most money. One field hand and his wife were sold to different bidders. There were tears in the woman's dark eyes as he was led away. She knew that she would never see her husband again.

"Let's get out of here," said Abe. "I can't stand any more."

They walked back to their own flatboat tied up at one of the wharves. Allen got supper, but Abe could not eat.

"Don't look like that," said Allen. "Many of the folks down here inherited their slaves, same as their land. Slavery ain't their fault."

"I never said it was anybody's fault — at least not anybody who's living now. But it just ain't right for one man to own another."

"Well, stop worrying. There's nothing you can do about it."

"Maybe not," said Abe gloomily, "but I'm mighty glad there aren't any slaves in Indiana."

Allen stayed on in New Orleans for several days to sell his cargo. It brought a good price. He then sold his flatboat, which would be broken up and used for lumber. Flatboats could not travel upstream. He and

Abe would either have to walk back to Indiana, or they could take a steamboat.

"We'd better not walk, carrying all this money," said Allen. "Pretty lonely country going home. We might get robbed."

The steamboat trip was a piece of good fortune that Abe had not expected. He enjoyed talking with the other passengers. The speed at which they traveled seemed a miracle. It had taken the boys a month to make the trip downstream by flatboat. They were returning upstream in little more than a week. They were standing together by the rail when the cabins of Rockport, perched on a high wooded bluff, came into view.

"It sure was good of your pa to give me this chance," said Abe. "I've seen some sights I wish I hadn't, but the trip has done me good. Sort of stretched my eyes and ears! Stretched me all over — inside, I mean." He laughed. "I don't need any stretching on the outside."

Allen looked at his tall friend. They had been together most of the time. They had talked with the same people, visited the same places, seen the same sights. Already Allen was beginning to forget them. Now that he was almost home, it was as if he had never been away.

But Abe seemed different. Somehow he had changed.

"I can't figure it out," Allen told him. "You don't seem the same."

"Maybe I'm not," said Abe. "I keep thinking about some of the things I saw."

CHAPTER *THIRTEEN*

THE LINCOLNS were leaving Pigeon Creek. One day a letter had arrived from John Hanks, a cousin, who had gone to Illinois to live. The soil was richer there, the letter said. Why didn't Tom come, too, and bring his family? He would find it easier to make a living. Even the name of the river near John's home had a pleasant sound. It was called the Sangamon, an Indian word meaning "plenty to eat."

"We're going," Tom decided. "I'm going to sell this farm and buy another. Do you want to come with us, Abe?"

Two years had passed since Abe's return from New Orleans. Two years of hard work. Two years of looking forward to his next birthday. He was nearly twenty-one and could leave home if he wanted to.

"Well, Pa — " he hesitated.

Sarah was watching him, waiting for his answer.

"I'll come with you," said Abe. "I'll stay long enough to help you get the new farm started."

There were thirteen people in the Lincoln party: Tom and Sarah, Abe and Johnny, Betsy and Dennis Hanks, who had been married for several years, Mathilda and her husband, and two sets of children. They made the journey in three big wagons, traveling over frozen roads and crossing icy streams. After two weeks they came to John Hanks' home on the prairies of Illinois. He made them welcome, then took them to see the place that he had selected for their farm. In the cold winter light it looked almost as desolate as Pigeon Creek had looked fourteen years before. Tom Lincoln was beginning all over again.

This time he had more help. John Hanks had a great pile of logs split and ready to be used for their new cabin. Abe was now able to do a man's work. After the cabin was finished, he split enough rails to build a fence around the farm. Some of the new neighbors hired him to split logs for them.

The following spring, he was offered other work that he liked much better. A man named Denton

Offut was building a flatboat, which he planned to float down the Illinois River to the Mississippi and on to New Orleans. He hired Abe to help with the cargo. The two young men became friends. When Abe returned home after the long voyage, he had news for Sarah.

"Ma," he said, "Denton is fixing to start a store up in New Salem. That's a village on the Sangamon River. He wants me to be his clerk."

Sarah said nothing for a moment. If Abe went away to stay, the cabin would seem mighty lonesome. She would miss him terribly. But she wanted him to do whatever was best for him.

"Mr. Offut said he'd pay me fifteen dollars a month," Abe added.

That was more money than he had ever earned, thought Sarah. And now that he was over twenty-one, he could keep his wages for himself. "I reckon you'll be leaving soon," she said aloud.

"Yes, Ma, I will." Telling her was harder than Abe had expected. "It is high time I start out on my own."

Sarah set to work to get his clothes ready. He was wearing his only pair of jeans, and there wasn't much else for him to take. She washed his shirts and the extra pair of socks that she had knit for him. He wrapped these up in a big cloth and tied the bundle to the end of a long stick. The next morning he was up early. After he told the rest of the family good-bye, Sarah walked with him to the gate.

Abe thrust the stick with his bundle over his shoulder. He had looked forward to starting out on his own, and now he was scared, almost as scared as he had felt on that cold winter afternoon when his new mother had first arrived in Pigeon Creek. Because she had believed in him, he had started believing in himself. Her faith in him was still shining in her eyes as she looked up at him and tried to smile.

He gave her a quick hug and hurried down the path.

It was a long, long walk to New Salem, where Abe arrived on a hot summer day in 1831. This village, on a high bluff overlooking the Sangamon River, was bigger than Gentryville, bigger even than Rockport. As he wandered up and down the one street, bordered on both sides by a row of neat log houses, he counted more than twenty-five buildings. There were several stores, and he could see the mill down by the river.

He pushed his way through a crowd that had gathered before one of the houses. A worried-looking man, about ten years older than Abe, sat behind a table on the little porch. He was writing in a big book.

"Howdy, mister," said Abe. "What is all the excitement about?"

"This is Election Day," the man replied, "and I am the clerk in charge. That is, I'm one of the clerks."

He stopped to write down the name of one of the men who stood in line. He wrote the names of several other voters in his big book before he had a chance to talk to Abe again. Then he explained that the other clerk who was supposed to help him was sick.

"I'm mighty busy," he went on. "Say listen, stranger, do you know how to write?"

"I can make a few rabbit tracks," Abe said, grinning.

"Maybe I can hire you to help me keep a record of the votes." The man rose and shook hands. "My name is Mentor Graham."

By evening the younger man and the older one had become good friends. Mr. Graham was a schoolmaster, and he promised to help Abe with his studies. Soon Abe began to make other friends. Jack Kelso took him fishing. Abe did not care much about fishing, but he liked to hear Jack recite poetry by Robert Burns and William Shakespeare. They were Jack's favorite poets, and they became Abe's favorites, too.

At the Rutledge Tavern, where Abe lived for a while, he met the owner's daughter, Ann Rutledge. Ann was sweet and pretty, with a glint of sunshine in her hair. They took long walks beside the river. It was easy to talk to Ann, and Abe told her some of his secret hopes. She thought that he was going to be a great man someday.

Her father, James Rutledge, also took an interest in him. Abe was invited to join the New Salem Debating Society. The first time that he got up to talk the other members expected him to spend the time telling funny stories. Instead he made a serious speech — and a very good one.

"That young man has more than wit and fun in his head," Mr. Rutledge told his wife that night.

Abe liked to make speeches, but he knew that he did not always speak correctly. One morning he was having breakfast at Mentor Graham's house. "I have a notion to study English grammar," he said.

"If you expect to go before the public," Mentor answered, "I think it the best thing you can do."

"If I had a grammar, I would commence now."

Mentor thought for a moment. "There is no one in

town who owns a grammar," he said finally. "But Mr. Vaner out in the country has one. He might lend you his copy."

Abe got up from the table and walked six miles to the Vaner farm. When he returned, he carried an open book in his hands. He was studying grammar as he walked.

Meanwhile he worked as a clerk in Denton Offut's store. Customers could buy all sorts of things there — tools and nails, needles and thread, mittens and calico, and tallow for making candles. One day a woman bought several yards of calico. After she left, Abe discovered that he had charged her six cents too much. That evening he walked six miles to give her the money. He was always doing things like that, and people began to call him "Honest Abe."

Denton was so proud of his clerk that he could not help boasting. "Abe is the smartest man in the United States," he said. "Yes, and he can beat any man in the country running, jumping, or wrastling."

Some rough fellows lived a few miles away in another settlement, called Clary Grove. "That Denton Offut talks too much with his mouth," they said angrily. They did not mind Abe being called smart. But they declared that no one could "outwrastle" their leader, Jack Armstrong. One day they rushed into the store and dared Abe to fight with Jack.

Abe laid down the book that he had been reading. "I don't hold with wooling and pulling," he said. "But if you want to fight, come on outside."

The Clary Grove boys soon realized that Denton's clerk was a good wrestler. Jack, afraid that he was going to lose the fight, stepped on Abe's foot with the sharp heel of his boot. The sudden pain made Abe angry. The next thing that Jack knew, he was being shaken back and forth until his teeth rattled. Then he was lying flat on his back in the dust.

Jack's friends let out a howl of rage. Several of them rushed at Abe, all trying to fight him at the same time. He stood with his back against the store, his fists doubled up. He dared them to come closer. Jack picked himself up.

"Stop it, fellows," he said. "I was beaten in a fair fight. If you ask me, this Abe Lincoln is the cleverest fellow that ever broke into the settlement."

From then on, Jack was one of Abe's best friends.

A short time later Abe enlisted as a soldier in the Black Hawk War to help drive the Indians out of Illinois. The Clary Grove boys were in his company,

and Abe was elected captain. Before his company had a chance to do any fighting, Blackhawk was captured in another part of Illinois, and the war was over.

When Abe came back to New Salem, he found himself out of a job. Denton Offut had left. The store had "winked out." Later, Abe and another young man, William Berry, decided to become partners. They borrowed money and started a store of their own.

One day a wagon piled high with furniture stopped out in front. A man jumped down and explained that he and his family were moving West. The wagon was too crowded, and he had a barrel of odds and ends that he wanted to sell. Abe, always glad to oblige, agreed to pay fifty cents for it. Later, when he opened it, he had a wonderful surprise.

The barrel contained a set of famous lawbooks. He had seen those same books in Mr. Pitcher's law office in Rockport. Now that he owned a set of his own, he could read any time he wished. Customers coming into the store usually found Abe lying on the counter, his nose buried in one of the new books. The more he read, the more interested he became.

Perhaps he spent too much time reading, instead of attending to business. William Berry was lazy, and not a very satisfactory partner. The store of Lincoln and Berry did so little business that it had to close. The partners were left with many debts to pay. Then Berry died, and "Honest Abe" announced that he would pay all of the debts himself, no matter how long it took.

For a while he was postmaster. A man on horseback brought the mail twice a week, and there were so few letters that Abe often carried them around in his hat until he could deliver them. He liked the job because it gave him a chance to read the newspapers to which the people in New Salem subscribed. But the pay was small, and he had to do all sorts of odd jobs to earn enough to eat. On many days he would have gone hungry if Jack Armstrong and his wife Hannah had not invited him to dinner. When work was scarce, he stayed with them two or three weeks at a time.

He knew that he had to find a way to earn more money, and he decided to study surveying. It was a hard subject, but he borrowed some books and read them carefully. He studied so hard that in six weeks' time he took his first job as a surveyor.

Sometimes when he was measuring a farm or laying out a new road, he would be gone for several weeks. People miles from New Salem knew who Abe Lincoln was. They laughed at him because he was so tall and awkward. They thought it funny that his trousers were always too short. But they also laughed at his jokes, and they liked him. He made so many new friends that he decided to be a candidate for the Illinois legislature.

One day during the campaign he had a long talk with Major John T. Stuart. Major Stuart had been Abe's commander in the Black Hawk War. He was now a lawyer in Springfield, a larger town twenty miles away.

"Why don't you study law?" he asked.

Abe pursed his lips. "I'd sure like to," he drawled; then added with a grin, "But I don't know if I have enough sense."

Major Stuart paid no attention to this last remark. "You have been reading law for pleasure," he went on. "Now go at it in earnest. I'll lend you the books you need."

This was a chance that Abe could not afford to miss. Every few days he walked or rode on horseback to Springfield to borrow another volume. Sometimes he read forty pages on the way home. He was twenty-five years old, and there was no time to waste.

Meanwhile he was making many speeches. He asked the voters in his part of Illinois to elect him to the legislature, which made the laws for the state. They felt that "Honest Abe" was a man to be trusted, and he was elected.

Late in November Abe boarded the stagecoach for the ride to Vandalia, then the capital of the state. He looked very dignified in a new suit and high plug hat. In the crowd that gathered to tell him good-bye, he could see many of his friends. There stood Coleman Smoot, who had lent him money to buy his new clothes. Farther back he could see Mr. Rutledge and

Ann, Hannah and Jack Armstrong, Mentor Graham, and others who had encouraged and helped him. And now he was on his way to represent them in the legislature. There was a chorus of "Good-bye, Abe."

Then, like an echo, the words came again in Ann's high, sweet voice: "Good-bye, Abe!" He leaned far out the window and waved.

He was thinking of Ann as the coach rolled over the rough road. He was thinking also of Sarah. If only she could see him now, he thought, as he glanced at the new hat resting on his knee.

CHAPTER *FOURTEEN*

THE LEGISLATURE MET for several weeks at a time. Between sessions, Abe worked at various jobs in New Salem and read his lawbooks. Most of his studying was done early in the morning and late at night. He still found time to see a great deal of Ann Rutledge. But this happiness was all too brief. That summer Ann died suddenly. Something of her gentle sweetness was to live on forever in his heart. After Ann died, he tried to forget his grief by studying harder than ever.

The year that he was twenty-eight he took his examination and was granted a lawyer's license. He decided to move to Springfield, which had recently been made the capital of the state.

It was a cold March day when he rode into this

thriving little town. He hitched his horse to the hitching rack in the public square and entered one of the stores. Joshua Speed, the owner, a young man about Abe's age, looked up with a friendly smile.

"Howdy, Abe," he said. "So you are going to be one of us?"

"I reckon so," Abe answered. "Say, Speed, I just bought myself a bedstead. How much would it cost me for a mattress and some pillows and blankets?"

Joshua took a pencil from behind his ear. He did some figuring on a piece of paper. "I can fix you up for about seventeen dollars."

Abe felt the money in his pocket. He had only seven dollars. His horse was borrowed, and he was still a thousand dollars in debt. Joshua saw that he was disappointed. He had heard Abe make speeches, and Abe was called one of the most promising young men in the legislature. Joshua liked him and wanted to know him better.

"Why don't you stay with me until you can do better?" he suggested. "I have a room over the store and a bed big enough for two."

A grin broke over Abe's homely features. "Good!" he said. "Where is it?"

"You'll find some stairs over there behind that pile of barrels. Go on up and make yourself at home."

Abe enjoyed living with Joshua Speed, and he enjoyed living in Springfield. He soon became as popular as he had once been in Pigeon Creek and in New Salem. As the months and years went by, more and more people came to him whenever they needed a lawyer to advise them. For a long time he was poor, but little by little he paid off his debts. With his first big fee he bought a quarter section of land for his stepmother, who had been so good to him.

The part of his work that Abe liked best was "riding the circuit." In the spring and again in the fall, he saddled Old Buck, his horse, and set out with a judge and several other lawyers to visit some of the towns close by. These towns "on the circuit" were too small to have law courts of their own. In each town the lawyers argued the cases and the judge settled the disputes that had come up during the past six months.

After supper they liked to gather at the inn to listen to Abe tell funny stories. "I laughed until I shook my ribs loose," said one dignified judge.

The other lawyers often teased Abe. "You ought to charge your clients more money," they said, "or you will always be as poor as Job's turkey."

One evening they held a mock trial. Abe was accused of charging such small fees that the other lawyers could not charge as much as they should. The judge looked as solemn as he did at a real trial.

"You are guilty of an awful crime against the pockets of your brother lawyers," he said severely. "I hereby sentence you to pay a fine."

There was a shout of laughter. "I'll pay the fine," said Abe good-naturedly. "But my own firm is never going to be known as 'Catchem and Cheatem.'"

Meanwhile a young lady named Mary Todd had come to Springfield to live. Her father was a rich and important man in Kentucky. Mary was pretty and well educated. Abe was a little afraid of her, but one night at a party he screwed up his courage to ask her for a dance.

"Miss Todd," he said, "I would like to dance with you the worst way."

As he swept her around the dance floor, he bumped into other couples. He stepped on her toes. "Mr. Lincoln," said Mary, as she limped over to a chair, "you did dance with me the worst way — the very worst."

She did not mind that he was not a good dancer. As she looked up into Abe's homely face, she decided that he had a great future ahead of him. She remembered something she had once said as a little girl: "When I grow up, I want to marry a man who will be President of the United States."

Abe was not the only one who liked Mary Todd. Among the other young men who came to see her was another lawyer, Stephen A. Douglas. He was no taller than Mary herself, but he had such a large head and shoulders that he had been nicknamed "the Little Giant." He was handsome and rich and brilliant. His friends thought that he might be President someday.

"No," said Mary, "Abe Lincoln has the better chance to succeed."

Anyway, Abe was the man she loved. The next year they were married.

"I mean to make him President of the United States," she wrote to a friend in Kentucky. "You will see that, as I always told you, I will yet be the President's wife."

At first Mary thought that her dream was coming true. In 1846 Abe was elected a member of the United States Congress in Washington. He had made a good start as a political leader, and she was disappointed when he did not run for a second term. Back he came to Springfield to practice law again. By 1854 there were three lively boys romping through the rooms of the comfortable white house that he had bought for his family. Robert was eleven, Willie was four, and Tad was still a baby. The neighbors used to smile to see Lawyer Lincoln walking down the street carrying Tad on his shoulders, while Willie clung to his coat-tails. The boys adored their father.

Mary did too, but she wished that Abe would be more dignified. He sat reading in his shirt sleeves, and he got down on the floor to play with the boys. His wife did not think that was any way for a successful lawyer to act. It also worried her that he was no longer interested in politics.

And then something happened that neither Mary nor Abe had ever expected. Their old friend, Stephen A. Douglas, who was now a Senator in Washington, suggested a new law. Thousands of settlers were going West to live, and in time they would form new states. The new law would make it possible for the people in each new state to own slaves, if most of the voters wanted to.

Abraham Lincoln was so aroused and indignant that he almost forgot his law practice. He traveled around Illinois making speeches. There were no laws against having slaves in the South, but slavery must be kept out of territory that was still free, he said. The new states should be places "for poor people to go to better their condition." Not only that, but it was wrong for one man to own another. Terribly wrong.

"If the Negro is a man," he told one audience, "then my ancient faith teaches me that all men are created equal."

Perhaps he was thinking of the first time he had visited a slave market. He was remembering the words in the Declaration of Independence that had thrilled him as a boy.

Two years later Abraham Lincoln was asked to be a candidate for the United States Senate. He would be running against Douglas. Abe wanted very much to be a Senator. Even more he wanted to keep slavery out of the new states. Taking part in the political campaign would give him a chance to say the things that he felt so deeply.

"I am convinced I am good enough for it," he told a friend, "but in spite of it all I am saying to myself every day, 'It is too big a thing for you; you will never get it.' Mary insists, however, that I am going to be Senator, and President of the United States, too."

Perhaps it was his wife's faith in him that gave him the courage to try. Never was there a more exciting campaign. Never had the people of Illinois been so stirred as during that hot summer of 1858. A series of debates was held in seven different towns. The two candidates — Douglas, "the Little Giant," and "Old Abe, the Giant Killer," as his friends called him — argued about slavery. People came from miles around to hear them.

On the day of a debate, an open platform for the speakers was decorated with red-white-and-blue bunting. Flags flew from the housetops. When Senator Douglas arrived at the railroad station, his friends and admirers met him with a brass band. He drove to his hotel in a fine carriage.

Abe had admirers, too. Sometimes a long procession met him at the station. Then Abe would be embarrassed. He did not like what he called "fizzlegigs and fireworks." But he laughed when his friends in one town drove him to his hotel in a hay wagon. This was their way of making fun of Stephen Douglas and his fine manners.

Senator Douglas was an eloquent orator. While he was talking, some of Abe's friends would worry. Would Old Abe be able to answer? Would he be able to hold his own? Then Abe would unfold his long legs and stand up. "The Giant Killer" towered so high above "the Little Giant" that a titter ran through the crowd.

When he came to the serious part of his speech, there was silence. His voice reached to the farthest corners of the crowd, as he reminded them what slavery really meant. He summed it up in a few words: "You work and toil and earn bread, and I'll eat it."

Both men worked hard to be elected. Douglas won. "I feel like the boy," said Abe, "who stubbed his toe. It hurts too bad to laugh, and I am too big to cry."

All of those who loved him — Mary, his wife, in her neat white house; Sarah, his stepmother, in her little cabin, more than a hundred miles away; and his many friends — were disappointed. But not for long. The part he took in the Lincoln-Douglas debates made his name known throughout the United States.

Abe Lincoln's chance was coming.

CHAPTER *FIFTEEN*

During the next two years Abraham Lincoln was asked to make many speeches. "Let us have faith that right makes might," he told one audience in New York, "and in that faith let us, to the end, dare to do our duty as we understand it."

At the end of the speech, several thousand people rose to their feet, cheering and waving their handkerchiefs. His words were printed in newspapers. Throughout the northern states, men and women began to think of him as the friend of freedom.

By 1860 he was so well known that he was nominated for President of the United States. Stephen A.

Douglas was nominated by another political party. Once more the two rivals were running for the same office.

Several thousands of Abraham Lincoln's admirers called themselves "Wide Awakes." There were Wide Awake Clubs in nearly every northern town. Night after night they marched in parades, carrying flaming torches and colored lanterns. And as they marched, they sang:

Hurrah! for our cause — of all causes the best!
Hurrah! for Old Abe, Honest Abe of the West.

No one enjoyed the campaign excitement more than did Willie and Tad Lincoln. They did their marching around the parlor carpet, singing another song:

Old Abe Lincoln came out of the wilderness,
Out of the wilderness, out of the wilderness,
Old Abe Lincoln came out of the wilderness,
    Down in Illinois.

People everywhere were talking about Old Abe, and he received a great deal of mail. Some of the letters came from Pigeon Creek. Nat Grigsby, his old schoolmate, wrote that his Indiana friends were thinking of him. Dave Turnham wrote. It was in Dave's book that Abe had first read the Declaration of Independence. A package arrived from Josiah Crawford, who had given him his *Life of Washington*. The package contained a piece of white oak wood. It was part of a rail that Abe had split when he was sixteen years old. Josiah thought that he might like to have it made into a cane.

Hundreds of other letters came from people he had never seen. One from New York State made him smile.

"I am a little girl only eleven years old," the letter read, "but want you should be President of the United States very much, so I hope you won't think me very bold to write to such a great man as you are. . . . I have got four brothers and part of them will vote for you anyway, and if you will let your whiskers grow I will try to get the rest of them to vote for you. You would look a great deal better, for your face is so thin. All the ladies like whiskers, and they would tease their husbands to vote for you and then you would be President. . . ."

The letter was signed "Grace Bedell." In less than two weeks she received an answer. Abraham Lincoln, who loved children, took her advice. By Election Day on November 6, 1860, he had started to grow a beard.

He spent the evening of Election Day in the telegraph office. Report after report came in from different parts of the country. He was gaining. He was winning. After a while he knew — his friends knew — all Springfield knew — that Abraham Lincoln was to be the next President of the United States. Outside in the streets the crowds were celebrating. They were singing, shouting, shooting off cannons. Abe told his friends that he was "well-nigh upset with joy."

"I guess I'd better go home now," he added. "There is a little woman there who would like to hear the news."

Mary was asleep when he entered their bedroom. Her husband touched her on the shoulder. "Mary, Mary," he said with a low chuckle, "we are elected."

By February the Lincolns were ready to move. Abe tied up the trunks and addressed them to "A. Lincoln, The White House, Washington, D.C." Before he left Illinois there was a visit he wanted to make to a log farmhouse a hundred and twenty-five miles southeast of Springfield. His father had been dead for ten years, but his stepmother was still living there.

Travel was slow in those days, and he had to change trains several times. There was plenty of time to think. He knew that hard days lay ahead. There were many Southerners who said that they were afraid to live under a President who was against slavery. Several southern states had left the Union and were starting a country of their own. For the United States to be broken up into two different nations seemed to him the saddest thing that could possibly happen. As President, Abraham Lincoln would have a chance — he must make the chance — to preserve the Union. He could not know then that he would also have a chance to free the slaves — a chance to serve his country as no other President had had since George Washington.

His thoughts went back to his boyhood. Even then he had wanted to be President. What had once seemed an impossible dream was coming true. He thought of all the people who had encouraged and helped him. He thought of his mother, who, more than any one person, had given him a chance to get ahead.

"Mother!" Whenever Abe said the word, he was thinking of both Nancy and Sarah.

Sarah was waiting by the window. A tall man in a high silk hat came striding up the path.

"Abe! You've come!" She opened the door and looked up into the sad, wise face.

"Of course, Mother." He gave her the kind of good bear hug he had given her when he was a boy. "I am leaving soon for Washington. Did you think I could go so far away without saying good-bye?"

The word spread rapidly that he was there. One after another, the neighbors dropped in, until the little room was crowded. As he sat before the fireplace, talking with all who came, Sarah seemed to see, not a man about to become President, but a forlorn-looking little boy. She had loved that little boy from the moment she first saw him. He had always been a good son to her — a better son than her own John.

When the last visitor had gone, she drew her chair closer. It was good to have a few minutes alone together.

"Abe," she told him, "I can say what scarcely one mother in a thousand can say."

He looked at her inquiringly.

"You never gave me a cross word in your life. I reckon your mind and mine, that is — " she laughed, embarrassed, "what little mind I had, seemed to run together."

He reached over and laid a big hand on her knee. She put her wrinkled, work-hardened hand on his.

When the time came to say good-bye, she could hardly keep the tears back. "Will I ever see you again?" she asked. "What if something should happen to you, Abe? I feel it in my heart — "

"Now, now, Mother." He held her close. "Trust in the Lord and all will be well."

"God bless you, Abraham."

He kissed her and was gone. "He was the best boy I ever saw," she thought, as she watched him drive away.